THE AGE OF BLISS

HASAN AND HUSAYN IBN ALI

ÖMER YILMAZ

NEW JERSEY • LONDON • FRANKFURT • CAIRO

TUGHRA
BOOKS

Copyright © 2017 by Tughra Books

19 18 17 16   2 3 4

All rights reserved. No part of this book may be reproduced or transmitted in any form or by any means, electronic or mechanical, including photocopying, recording or by any information storage and retrieval system without permission in writing from the Publisher.

Translated by Asiye Gülen
Edited by Clare Duman

Published by Tughra Books
345 Clifton Ave., Clifton,
NJ, 07011, USA
www.tughrabooks.com

Library of Congress Cataloging-in-Publication Data Available

ISBN: 978-1-59784-378-2

TABLE OF CONTENTS

Hasan and Husayn ibn Ali

Respected Hasan

*I*t was three years since the great migration (*Hijra*) and Fatima, may Allah be pleased with her, was nearing the end of her pregnancy with Hasan, may Allah be pleased with him. When she went into labor, the blessed Prophet sent his wife to her, saying: "To help Fatima give birth easily, recite Ayat al-Kursi, an-Nas, al-Falaq and say also the following: Indeed your Lord is Allah. He created the heavens and the earth in six days and makes the night give way to day. The whole of creation is His and even the sun, moon and stars obey Him. Praise Allah, the King of the Universe."

After a short and easy labor, Fatima gave birth to a beautiful boy. Soon she was visited by the noble Prophet who said: "Show me my grandson. What is his name?"

Ali ibn Abi Talib, may Allah be pleased with him, the child's father, was a man of great courage who bravely fought against evil, so he wanted to call his son Harb, meaning "battle."

However, this name did not meet with the beloved Prophet's approval and he gave the child a hitherto unknown name, "Hasan." The Messenger of Allah had good reason for choosing a child's name carefully and explained: "On the Day of Judgment, you will be called by your names, and your fathers' names, so you should choose excellent names."

The noble Prophet then took his grandchild, Hasan, lovingly in his arms and recited the *adhan* in his right ear and the *iqamah* in his left.

Aqiqah

To give thanks for the safe arrival of a newborn child, a celebration called *Aqiqah* takes place, anytime between birth and puberty, but usually within a week or so of the birth. *Aqiqah* means the hair of a newborn child, which is shaved off, weighed, and an equal weight in gold is given away to someone in need. The baby's name can also be announced at this ceremony.

Aisha, may Allah be pleased with her, the noble Prophet's wife, said that the Messenger of Allah encouraged the sacrifice of *Aqiqah* for a newborn baby.

Before Islam, it was the custom in Arabian culture to celebrate this sacrifice only for baby boys, but such is the beauty of Islam that it gives great importance also to the birth of girls.

The blessed Prophet told Fatima to give silver weighing the same as the child's hair to somebody in need as a charitable act. He also said that *Aqiqah* should take place within a week of birth, so as to safeguard the child from misfortune and mishap.

Resemblance

*I*n the same way as his mother, Fatima, Hasan looked very much like the noble Prophet. One day, when the Messenger of Allah was out for a walk with Abu Bakr, may Allah be pleased with him, and Ali, they saw Hasan. Abu Bakr lifted Hasan onto his shoulders and said: "It's beyond belief how much you look like your grandfather, rather than your father!"

Hasan's father, Ali ibn Abi Talib, smiled at these words.

Even Hasan's mother, Fatima, when putting him to bed, would say: "My dear child, you look so much like your grandfather, but not at all like your father."

Even the noble Prophet's best friends said that the person who most resembles the Messenger of Allah is his grandson, Hasan. One day, they were discussing the subject when Abdullah ibn Zubayr, may Allah be pleased with him, came along, so they asked him: "What is your opinion on this subject?"

Abdullah ibn Zubayr replied: "The person who looks most like the blessed Prophet is the one he loves most—his grandson, Hasan."

Flowers of the Messenger of Allah

The blessed Prophet loved his grandchildren, Hasan and Husayn, may Allah be pleased with him, very much and sometimes sat them on his shoulders.

One day, Abu Ayyub al-Ansari, may Allah be pleased with him, visited the noble Prophet's house and saw him playing with Hasan and Husayn. He wanted to know: "O Messenger of Allah, do you really love them that much?"

The beloved Prophet replied: "How could I not love them? They smell as sweet as the basil that grows in the earth."

Sermon (Khutba)

One day the blessed Prophet was preaching when Hasan and Husayn arrived at the mosque, but were being difficult. Upon seeing his grandchildren, the noble Prophet interrupted his sermon, took the boys in his arms and placed them in front of him. Then he explained: "Allah says: your possessions and your children will tempt and try you. Allah speaks the truth—when I saw these two, I couldn't resist them."

On another occasion, the Messenger of Allah was preaching with Hasan sitting on his knees. At one and the same time, he was both appealing to his congregation, while kissing Hasan and saying that he loved him.

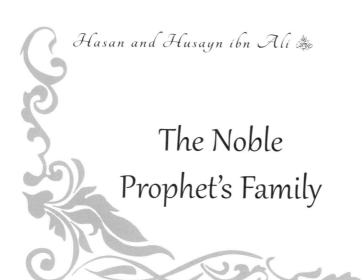

The Noble Prophet's Family

mm Salama, may Allah be pleased with her, wife of the Messenger of Allah, addressed her family, saying: "The verses, 'Allah wishes only to cleanse you from all evil and make you wholly pure' were revealed at my house. Fatima, Ali, Hasan and Husayn were all present."

Then, Allah's Messenger wrapped them in his cloak and said: 'These are my family (*Ahl al-Bayt*). That is why Allah wishes only to cleanse them from evil and make them wholly pure.'"

At another time, the noble Prophet raised his hands and prayed as follows: "O Allah! These are my family and my relatives. Remove from them all evil and make them wholly pure."

Whenever he passed by Fatima's house on his way to pray, the Messenger of Allah always said: "O my family, it is time to pray" and he recited this verse: "O family of the Messenger of Allah! Allah wishes only to cleanse you from all evil, and make you wholly pure."

Again, they were close by a water fountain called Humm one day, when the noble Prophet stood up to address his Companions. After giving thanks to Allah, he continued: "I am also a human being like you and, like all mortals, I will die. But I shall leave two things to help you. First is the Book of Allah, which contains guidance and light. For that reason, cling to Allah's Book and obey Him. Second, I leave with you my family (*Ahl al-Bayt*). They will remind you of Allah's ways."

The significance of loving the blessed Prophet's family is stated in the Qur'an: "*Say: 'I ask for no reward for teaching you Allah's religion, only that you love my family members'.*" (ash-Shura 42:23).

In this verse "family members" refers to our Prophet's family (*Ahl al-Bayt*). His family is Fatima, Ali, Hasan, and Husayn.

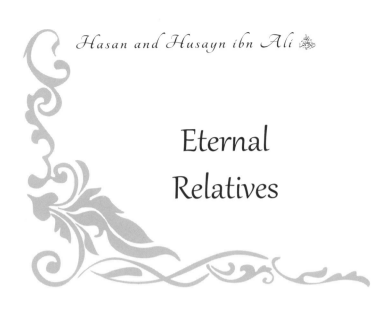
Eternal Relatives

On this subject, the noble Prophet said: "On the Day of Judgment, all family bonds will come to an end, with each child being ascribed to his father. My family bonds alone will not end, but Fatima's children, Hasan and Husayn will be ascribed to me."

With these words, our Prophet demonstrated just how much he loved Hasan and Husayn.

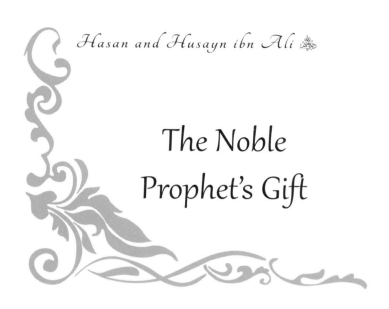

The Noble Prophet's Gift

Once, the blessed Prophet was visiting his daughter when Hasan and Husayn were in bed asleep. Hasan woke up thirsty, so the Messenger of Allah got a glass of water. He was about to give it to Hasan when Husayn woke up, too, and tried to take the water to drink. The beloved Prophet gave the glass to Hasan, whereupon Fatima, who saw what was happening, remarked: "I think you love Hasan more than Husayn."

The Messenger of Allah denied this, saying: "No, Hasan asked for the water first."

Another time, the noble Prophet came to see Fatima and Ali ibn Abi Talib. Hasan and Husayn were very thirsty, but their father was sleeping, so the Messenger of Allah got up and drew milk from Ali's sheep, which he then gave to Hasan to drink. Fatima said to her father: "O Allah's Messenger! I think you love Hasan more than Husayn."

The blessed Prophet replied: "No! Hasan asked first, so I gave it to him."

Then the noble Prophet gave Fatima some good news: "You and I will be together before Allah on the Day of Judgment."

Diversions during Prayer Time

The blessed Prophet was never happier than when he was performing the Prescribed Prayers. As a rule, time flew by when he was absorbed in Prayer, without him even noticing. Even Aisha was unable to explain this to people who asked her.

However, one thing couldn't fail to disturb the noble Prophet's Prayers, and that was his grandchildren, Hasan and Husayn. There was the time when, seeing his grandfather prostrated in Prayer, Hasan climbed onto his shoulders, but the Messenger of Allah stayed where he was until Hasan was ready to climb off.

On another occasion, Hasan again climbed onto his grandfather's shoulders while he was prostrated, but it was only when the noble Prophet stood up after the *ruku* (bending) that Hasan climbed off him.

Sometimes the people around the blessed Prophet were critical of his love for his grandchildren. On one occasion, when Hasan and Husayn were sitting on his shoulders as he was praying, the crowd tried to intervene, but the beloved Prophet signaled for them not to interfere. When the Prayer was finished, the Messenger of Allah took the boys in his arms and said: "Whoever loves me, should love these two also."

The noble Prophet came to the mosque one day with Hasan perched on his shoulders. He began to pray and during his Prayers he was prostrated for a very long time. Afterwards people asked him why it was so long.

"O Messenger of Allah, we've never seen you prostrate for so long before. Was it because of a divine command, or divine inspiration?"

The blessed Prophet answered: "No, it was for neither of these reasons. My dear child was on my shoulders, so I waited for him to finish his game."

Hasan and Husayn ibn Ali ﷺ

The Noble Prophet's Love for His Grandchildren

O ne day the Messenger of Allah was out walking with Hasan riding on his shoulders. One of his Companions saw them and said to Hasan: "O Hasan! What a beautiful mount you have there!"

The blessed Prophet replied: "Hasan is a good rider."

Another day, the beloved Prophet put the boys on his back and walked on his arms, saying to them: "What a good camel you have, and what clever riders you are."

When Umar, may Allah be pleased with him, saw them he said: "How precious your horse is!"

The Messenger of Allah replied: "They are good riders too."

Allah said: "If it were not for you, Muhammad, I would not have created the world." But the noble Prophet was not upset to be called a horse, or any other mount. He was just being human, like any other person.

Expression
of Love

as has been noted before, some people found the noble Prophet's obvious love for Hasan a bit strange. One of them saw him kiss Hasan on the cheek and said to him: "I have ten children and have never kissed any of them so far."

The Messenger of Allah responded: "Those who do not show mercy, will be shown no mercy."

The blessed Prophet tried to teach us how to relate to people in society. If we seek love from other people, we need to show them love. If we seek respect ourselves, then we have to respect the rights of others.

The Noble Prophet's Prayers

The Messenger of Allah used to pray night and day for those he loved.

Usama, may Allah be pleased with him, remembers: "The Messenger of Allah had me on one of his knees, and Hasan on the other and he was cuddling us both and saying: 'O Allah, bless these two, because I care greatly for both of them'."

It is said that the noble Prophet used to pray for Hasan in the same way: "O Allah! I love him! You, love him, too! Love the ones who love him!"

These ways in which the beloved Prophet prayed are good examples for Muslim people to follow. If we love the noble Prophet, we must also love his beloved Hasan. Thus it was that one of his Companions took on himself the mission of delivering this message to humanity. That person was Ali and he was martyred. Society was sliding into chaos, as Hasan had predicted. He went into the pulpit (*mimbar*) and spoke to the people. At the same time, a member of the community stood up and supported Hasan, saying:

"I have seen the Messenger of Allah embracing Hasan while saying: 'Love me, love him.' He also wanted this message to reach others outside the community, otherwise I would not be standing and addressing you now."

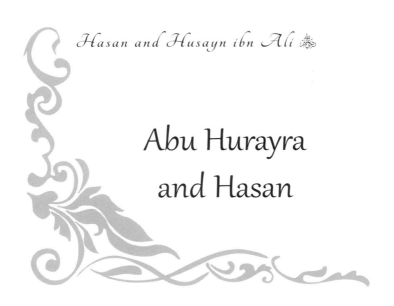

Abu Hurayra
and Hasan

bu Hurayra, may Allah be pleased with him, who belonged to the noble Prophet's group of Companions, used to burst into tears whenever he saw Hasan, because he reminded him so much of the blessed Prophet.

He remembered one time when he and the beloved Prophet met in the mosque and decided to go into town together to see if they could find Hasan. The Messenger of Allah was quiet, probably because he was thinking about his dearest grandchild, Hasan. They could not find Hasan so, after a few minutes walking, they came back to the mosque, but still could not find Hasan.

Aisha thought it likely that Hasan's mother had bathed him and he was still getting dressed. But the noble Prophet asked Abu Hurayra to go and fetch Hasan. When he appeared, he and the Messenger of Allah fell into each other's arms with great joy. Then Hasan began to play with the blessed Prophet's beard.

The Messenger of Allah showed his great love with a kiss and a prayer for him: "O Allah, I love him so much. You love him, too. Love everyone who loves him as well."

On another day, while Hasan was still a child, Abu Hurayra met him and said: "Pull up your shirt. I want to kiss you in the same place the Messenger of Allah did."

Hasan pulled up his shirt and Abu Hurayra kissed him on his belly.

Abu Hurayra told a story about how much the noble Prophet loved his grandchildren: "In the days when the Messenger of Allah used to carry Hasan on one shoulder and Husayn on the other, he was walking towards us and just kept kissing the boys all the time."

We said: "O Messenger of Allah, you obviously love them greatly."

The noble Prophet replied: "Yes, I do. Anyone who loves them, loves me: anyone who bears a grudge against them, bears a grudge against me."

Prayer Times

asan went to the mosque early each morning to perform the Morning Prayer with the community, and then stayed on until dawn to honor Allah and take part in a period of instruction. He believed this routine would safeguard a person from damnation.

At dawn, Hasan would spend an hour or so chatting with people arriving at the mosque, before performing his Morning Prayer, after which he would drop in on the noble Prophet's wife on his way home to ask if all was well with them.

Whilst everyone is exhorted to make pilgrimage to the Ka'ba once in their lifetime, Hasan's high regard for the Ka'ba was demonstrated by the number of times he walked there as a pilgrim.

Even this was not enough for him—he wanted also to provide food in support of other pilgrims. One day, a group of wealthy pilgrims visited Hasan and even these people he wanted to support, but they said they had no need of help. However, Hasan was insistent, saying: "Allah will be certain to point out those who help others to the angels, saying: 'These wrongdoers came here for My sake, with contrite hearts, to seek My forgiveness. See, I forgive all their sins.'"

Hasan went on: "By providing you with food for your pilgrimage, I am trying to please Allah and seek His forgiveness."

Hasan loved to perform kind acts for other people. He always used to donate his excess wealth to those in need. For example, if he had two pairs of shoes, he would give one pair to a poor person and keep the other for himself. If he had two plates of food, he would give one to the poor.

Ali had announced to a crowd of people that Hasan had some belongings which he wanted to share out. Hearing this, a big crowd formed, so Hasan stood up and added: "People! I want to share my belongings only with the poor."

Hearing these words, nearly half of the crowd melted away. Ash'as ibn Qays, may Allah be pleased with him, was one of those who received a share of his belongings.

Hasan and Peace

Hasan was a tender-hearted person. He gave great importance to peace within his society, and didn't want political ideologies to split the people and incite them to murder each other. He had heard the noble Prophet's statement about this. One day, the Messenger of Allah was praying and Hasan came in and jumped over his shoulders while he was prostrated. The blessed Prophet raised his head very slowly, so as not to hurt Hasan. This was repeated several times and a Companion of the beloved Prophet was surprised and asked: "O Messenger of Allah! Why have you not played with other children as you play with Hasan?"

The noble Prophet replied: "This son is sacred. Allah will bring peace between two nations through Hasan."

The blessed Prophet was foretelling an event which would take place years into the future, when Hasan would renounce the caliphate in order to bring peace between nations, just as the beloved Prophet had predicted.

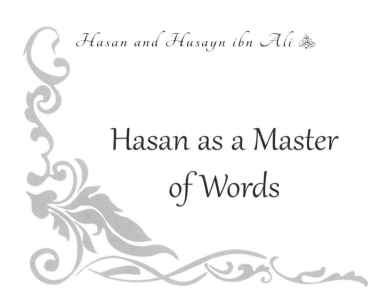

Hasan as a Master of Words

Hasan was a good preacher, able to express his thoughts and words very well; something which made his brother Husayn jealous of him. He also stood as an example of high moral standards. He would prefer not to speak, but rather to listen, if his father were present at a gathering. Once, Ali asked him to preach to the community.

Hasan told his father: "I would never preach to people in front of you."

But Ali insisted he preached to the community, saying, "Then I will listen to you from a dark corner where you cannot see me."

Hasan stood up, gave thanks, praised Allah, and preached to the community. Ali contentedly enjoyed his speech. As Hasan descended from the pulpit, Ali softly recited the following Qur'anic verse: "*Allah is the One who knows and deals with everything fairly. Allah chose Adam, Noah, Abraham's family and Imran's lineage to follow each other respectively, and made them great among all peoples*" (Al Imran 3:33). The verse pointed towards future pious generations that would be born through the noble Prophet's family. Hasan's preaching was also valued for its clarity of expression and avoidance of offensive words.

Sunset

Hasan was only eight years old when the noble Prophet passed away, so he remembered few things the Messenger of Allah said. One exception concerned the accidental eating of a date given as alms. The story is related by one of the Companions: "We were sitting with the blessed Prophet one day when someone came in with a plate of alms and offered it around."

The beloved Prophet immediately asked: "Are you offering this as a gift or as alms?"

The man replied: "As alms."

In his generosity, the noble Prophet offered the plate to the community, because he could not accept alms. However, Hasan, being only a child, had quickly taken a date and put it in his mouth, whereupon the blessed Prophet, even more quickly, had removed it.

People in the room were really surprised: "O Messenger of Allah, why did you remove the date from his mouth?"

The noble Prophet said to his grandson: "Hasan, taking an alms offering is not allowed for our family."

Another of the blessed Prophet's sayings, which Hasan remembered was: "If you have doubts about something, avoid it and do what you know is right. Doing wrong will undermine your confidence; doing what is right will bolster your confidence."

Prayers

The beloved Prophet also used to teach his dear grandchild, Hasan, how to pray and this is one of the prayers he remembered: "Dear Allah, make me one of those people who follows the true path, who enjoys their meals, who You love. Help me avoid what is forbidden, and always provide me with whatever blessings You know I need. Someone You love can never be a wrongdoer. O Allah, how great You are!"

From Hasan's birth to the noble Prophet's death, eight years later, the two of them spent a lot of time together. During this period, we learn a lot about how the blessed Prophet related to Hasan, playing with him, teaching him to pray, and educating him in his religion. It's never too soon to learn about Islam and Allah's delights in the prayers of children.

At dawn, Hasan prayed: "Thanks to Allah who is great! All things belong to Allah! He is the only Allah! Allah has power over everything!"

Hasan's Advice
to Children

One day, Hasan called the boys around and talked to them like this: "Kids! Right now, you are little children, but one day you will be grownups. It is important that you acquire knowledge. If you can memorize information, do it: if you cannot memorize, write it down and learn it somehow."

Hasan's Character

Hasan spoke well about the meaning of morality and the importance of sharing with other people. He defined morality as being honest and well-mannered and protecting other peoples' rights, especially with regard to relatives. Morality also means sharing what you have with others, being in awe of Allah, and wary of mortal beings.

Caliphate Times

*P*eople who were not happy under the caliphate of Ali plotted to assassinate him. According to this plan, an unfortunate person named Ibn Muljam was to murder him. Accordingly, he followed Ali and planned to ambush him on his way to the mosque for the Morning Prayer. When he saw his target, he attacked and wounded him. Ali was bleeding profusely but, despite this, was exhorting the community not to miss the Prayer time.

Ali called for his son, Hasan, and said: "If I live, I may forgive or punish him. If I die, you punish him. But do not overstep the mark, and do not make a Muslim bleed. (Allah definitely does not admire those who overstep the mark.")

His condition was getting worse. When the community realized the situation, they asked Ali: "If the worst happens, should we pick your son Hasan as the caliph?"

Just as the noble Prophet before him, Ali didn't want to talk about this subject with them, so he called his sons Hasan and Husayn over and gave them some advice: ("Sons! Fear Allah. Be honest all the time. Show mercy to orphans. Live a good life, mindful of the afterlife. Help people in trouble. Rise up against bad people, and help good ones. Follow the Qur'an in all things. Live a good life and earn Allah's favor.")

All of this advice was intended as a lesson for Hasan.

Then Ali passed away.

When Ali died a martyr in this way, the people swore loyalty to Hasan, who was chosen as the fifth caliph.

After becoming caliph, Hasan preached a lengthy sermon in the mosque. Then he commanded that

Ibn Muljam, his father's murderer, be brought before him. Hasan punished him after listening to his defense. But the people who hadn't wanted Ali as caliph, didn't want Hasan either. Hasan instinctively realized that this situation could result in a divided society, with Muslim fighting Muslim, which he did not want. So he agreed to stand aside for Muawiya to become the next caliph.

Hasan explained why he left the caliphate to Muawiya in this way: "A wise person fears Allah: a foolish person is one who does not hesitate to sin. I just wanted this society to stay in peace and to stay united. I did not want anyone to be killed. These are the reasons why I left the caliphate to Muawiya."

In doing this, the noble Prophet's prediction had come true. He had said, even when Hasan was just a child: "This son of mine is a *sayyid* (chief). I hope Allah may reconcile two parties of my community by means of him."

After his resignation as caliph, Hasan headed towards Medina, and the people of Kufa (Iraq) were crying as he left the city.

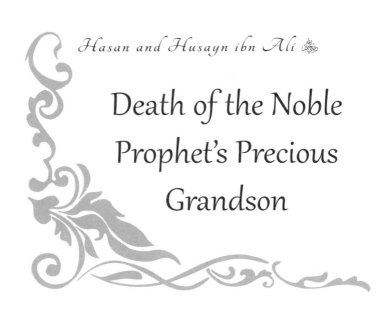

Death of the Noble Prophet's Precious Grandson

Having lived another ten years in Medina, Hasan sent a message to Aisha asking to be buried next to the blessed Prophet, and Aisha gave her consent to this kind request.

Hasan then told his last will to his beloved sister: "I have asked Aisha for permission to be buried next to the Messenger of Allah. She has agreed, but you'd better remind her. If anyone tries to block this burial, do not fight against them—just bury me in Al-Baqi Cemetery."

Hasan lived, bed-ridden, until the year 670, and was then buried in Al-Baqi Cemetery. The governor, at Husayn's request, performed the Funeral Prayer, in the presence of a huge crowd.

Respected Husayn

bbas's wife, Umm Fadl, may Allah be pleased with her, had a dream that a piece of the noble Prophet's body had been put in her house. This dream so upset her that she told the Messenger of Allah about it.

The blessed Prophet interpreted this dream: "Fatima will bear a baby boy, and you are going to breastfeed him."

It was four years after the migration to Medina (*Hijra*), when Husayn, the grandchild of the noble Prophet was born and the dream came true. Umm Fadl took the baby into her home and breastfed him.

Name

The Messenger of Allah gave the baby the name of Husayn by reciting the *adhan* into his ear. Ali had wanted to name this baby Harb as with Hasan, but the noble Prophet picked the name Husayn for him. Husayn's first morsel was a date, which was given to him by the blessed Prophet himself.

Aqiqah

Seven days after Husayn's birth, the noble Prophet sacrificed a ram to celebrate *Aqiqah*. The Messenger of Allah requested that a piece of the meat be delivered to the nurse who had helped at Husayn's birth. As for the rest of the meat, one third should be donated to the poor and the rest eaten at the family meal.

Then, the noble Prophet called for his daughter: "Fatima! Cut the baby's hair and donate coins to the poor, equivalent to his hair weight."

As requested, Fatima carried out this order quickly and donated silver coins weighing the same as Husayn's hair weight.

Resemblance

*J*ust like Hasan, Husayn bore a remarkable resemblance to the beloved Prophet.

His father, Ali, said: "Hasan's resemblance to the Messenger of Allah is from chest to head, whereas Husayn's similarities are all the rest of his body."

Playing Tag

One of the Companions had invited the blessed Prophet for dinner. On his way to his friend's house, the noble Prophet came across Husayn playing with his friends outside. The blessed Prophet tried to hug Husayn but the boy began to run away, which made the beloved Prophet smile. Soon, he caught up with Husayn, hugged him, gave him a kiss and said: "Husayn is with me, and I am with Husayn."

The Messenger of Allah was trying to express how much he loved Husayn, at the same time implying that anyone who hurts Husayn, hurts the noble Prophet.

The Noble Prophet's Sensitivity

O ne day, the Messenger of Allah came to his daughter, Fatima, and asked: "Where are my boys?"

He meant, of course, his grandchildren, Hasan and Husayn. Fatima replied: "There was nothing in the kitchen for them to eat first thing this morning, so Ali suggested he take them for a walk, and he did."

When the noble Prophet caught up with them, he saw his grandchildren playing behind some date palms. It was blistering hot outside and the blessed Prophet was worried about them playing in such weather.

He asked his son-in-law, Ali: "Ali, shouldn't you have taken them home before it got too hot?"

Ali replied: "There was nothing for them to eat first thing this morning, so I picked some dates for them. If it's alright with you, I'll pick some for Fatima as well."

Once Ali had picked some more dates, they all began to walk home. The noble Prophet was unhappy about his grandchildren walking in this temperature, so he put one of them on his back, and the other went on Ali's back. After a while, they swapped these precious loads.

The Noble Prophet's Tolerance

The Messenger of Allah called round to see Husayn when he was with his wet-nurse, Umm Fadl, because he wanted to see him being breastfed by her.

When the child was full, he took him on his lap. But this little boy had a surprise for his grandfather; he threw up on him and made his shirt wet! The beloved Prophet didn't mind; he just changed his shirt.

Maternal Feeling

hen Husayn was a young baby, he had a disease that made him cry all night long, which meant that Fatima couldn't get any sleep herself. One day, Husayn had fallen asleep towards morning, so Fatima, having performed the Morning Prayer, went back to bed to sleep. The noble Prophet visited Fatima after he had performed the Morning Prayer and, seeing Fatima asleep, thought she had missed the Prayers.

"My lovely daughter, don't ever think that just by virtue of being the noble Prophet's daughter, you can omit to perform your Prayers. I swear to Allah, Who has appointed me to be His last Prophet, you will not enter Paradise unless you perform your Prayers."

Love of Children

The noble Prophet couldn't bear to hear his grandchildren crying, because he always thought they should get what they wanted. When they cried, it really hurt him, because he loved them so much. If he heard a child crying, he would try to finish his Prayers quickly to let the mothers get back to their children.

It is almost impossible to explain in simple words just how much he loved Husayn.

Once, the Messenger of Allah explained his love for Husayn with these words: "If a person loves Husayn, he loves Allah."

This is what he meant by this phrase: love of Husayn comes from love of the blessed Prophet. Love of the beloved Prophet comes from love of Allah.

There is also evidence of the noble Prophet's love for his daughter, Fatima, namely, when he said: "Fatima is a piece of me."

But the Messenger of Allah loved Husayn in a different way. Once, the blessed Prophet saw Husayn crying and he berated his mother, Fatima, saying: "Don't you know I can't bear to hear that child crying?"

Another day he was asked who he loved most, and he replied: "Hasan and Husayn."

When the noble Prophet wanted to see his grandchildren he would say to Fatima: "Call my boys over!"

Then, when they had come, he would smell their bodies and cuddle them.

One night, at midnight, Osama found the noble Prophet outside, wrapped in a blanket. He was curious and asked the blessed Prophet: "O Messenger of Allah, what is wrong with this blanket?"

The beloved Prophet removed the blanket and two little boys popped out! They were Hasan and Husayn, of course! The noble Prophet said: "These are my boys. I love them so much. Allah, please love them and love those who love them."

The Messenger of Allah had talked to his family, including Husayn: "I fight against the ones who are fighting against you. I live in peace with the ones who are at peace with you."

Another time, he said: "Those who love me, Hasan, Husayn and their parents will be with me on the Day of Judgment."

The Noble Prophet's Line of Descent

rabs living in the pre-Islamic Age of Ignorance (*Jahiliyya*) did not want to have daughters because they felt ashamed of having baby girls. If someone had a daughter, he would bury the baby alive so as not to feel shame in society.

The Qur'an says this on the subject: "*When people are gifted with a baby girl, they feel shame and hide what they consider to be their bad news! So they have to choose—either to keep the baby alive and live in shame, or to bury the baby alive. Just see how often they make the bad choice!*" (an-Nahl 16:58–59).

People wanted boys to take over from their fathers eventually as head of the family and to take care of family members. It was Allah's Will that the noble Prophet's sons would not survive into manhood, but because he did not have a son to continue his line, non-believers nicknamed him *abtar*, which means infertile. But Allah promised the blessed Prophet, as proclaimed in Surah al-Kawthar (abundance), that his line would continue to flourish through his daughter, Fatima, and her sons, Hasan and Husayn.

People descended from Hasan were called "Sharif" or "Amir," while those from Husayn's line were called "Sayyid" which means "leader." The beloved Prophet used to say that Husayn would be the "sayyid" of humanity on Judgment Day. Friday is defined as the "sayyid" of the week.

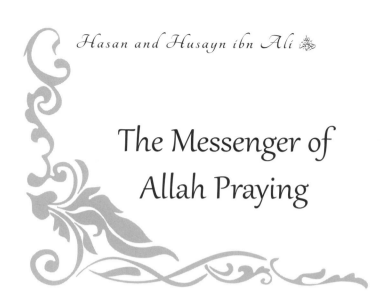

Hasan and Husayn ibn Ali ﷺ

The Messenger of Allah Praying

The noble Prophet always used to pray for Hasan and Husayn.

One day, he said: "Bring my boys here, and I will pray for them in the way Abraham prayed for his boys, Isaac and Ishmael."

When they came, the blessed Prophet embraced them and prayed: "I seek the protection of Allah because of wickedness and evil eyes."

After saying this prayer, the beloved Prophet remarked: "Abraham used to pray for Ishmael and Isaac in this way."

Wrestling Matches

When Hasan and Husayn began wrestling, the noble Prophet would watch them, and say: "Go for it, Hasan. Let me see your skills."

Ali was surprised because the noble Prophet was supporting Hasan, who was older than Husayn and said: "O Messenger of Allah! Shouldn't you support Husayn?"

The beloved Prophet replied: "Look, the Archangel Gabriel supports Hasan as well."

Running

One day, Hasan and Husayn were competing against each other at running. The noble Prophet had embraced them both and said: "Having kids leads a person to meanness and cowardliness."

What the Messenger of Allah was trying to say was that when someone has children, he may have to be careful with money in order to provide for the children's needs. In the same way, a parent is afraid of dying, not because of wishing to live longer, but because the children need looking after.

Leaders of Youth in Paradise

The Angel Gabriel brought news to the blessed Prophet that Hasan and Husayn had been chosen to be leaders of youth in Paradise. The noble Prophet was overjoyed at the news of his grandchildren's great position in Paradise, and he sometimes alluded to it.

One day, Husayn went to the mosque and the beloved Prophet showed him to the people and said: "If you wish to see the leader of youth in Paradise, here he is."

The Messenger of Allah did not share just the news relating to Hasan and Husayn; he also spoke about his son-in-law, Ali: "Hasan and Husayn have been appointed leaders of youth in Paradise, but their father will be an even greater leader than they."

Umar's Loyalty

The noble Prophet had died and Umar had succeeded as caliph after Abu Bakr. The council met to decide how incomes should be shared. When it came to Hasan and Husayn, Umar wanted them to be paid the same as others who took part in the Battle of Badr. Umar got his wish and thus repaid the blessed Prophet's love of Hasan and Husayn with his loyalty.

Abu Hurayra's Loyalty

hen Abu Hurayra, may Allah be pleased with him, was referring to the love that the noble Prophet felt for Husayn, he would say: "Don't argue with me. If people knew the good things I know about you, they would carry you aloft in triumph."

Husayn commanded the respect not only of Abu Hurayra. One day, a group of people, including the blessed Prophet's friend Amr ibn As, may Allah be pleased with him, were sitting around the Ka'ba.

Amr said something like this: "In our age, Husayn is the nicest human being on earth, according to the angels in the sky."

Praying

During the Witr Prayer, Husayn would pray in this way: "O Allah, only You see all things, but no one can see You. Nothing escapes Your gaze. Both Earth and Heavens belong to You. We seek Your protection to avoid disgrace."

Passing Away

One day the Angel Gabriel had visited the noble Prophet and asked Umm Salama, may Allah be pleased with her: "Umm Salama, please shut the door and don't let anyone come in."

Husayn was running towards the door and although Umm Salama tried to prevent him entering, she could not. Running into the room, little Husayn found himself in the noble Prophet's arms, kissed and hoisted to his shoulder.

When Gabriel saw this demonstration of love, he asked: "Do you love him that much?"

The Messenger of Allah answered: "Yes."

Then Gabriel said: "He will be murdered by your people."

The noble Prophet was shocked and sorrowful for his grandchild. It was devastating for him to know that Husayn would be killed by people from his own Islamic nation.

Gabriel suggested: "Shall I show you where he is to be murdered?"

When the blessed Prophet was shown the terrain of Karbala, he could not hold back his tears.

The noble Husayn was martyred there in 680.